APR -- 2014

jB
YOUSAFZA
I
Rowell, Rebecca,
author.

Malala Yousafzai.

$34.22

DATE			

MALALA
YOUSAFZAI

Education Activist

MALALA
YOUSAFZAI

Education Activist

BY REBECCÄ ROWELL

CONTENT CONSULTANT
ANITA ANANTHARAM
ASSISTANT PROFESSOR
CENTER FOR WOMEN'S STUDIES
AND GENDER RESEARCH
UNIVERSITY OF FLORIDA

ABDO
Publishing Company

CREDITS

Published by ABDO Publishing Company, PO Box 398166, Minneapolis, MN 55439. Copyright © 2014 by Abdo Consulting Group, Inc. International copyrights reserved in all countries. No part of this book may be reproduced in any form without written permission from the publisher. The Essential Library™ is a trademark and logo of ABDO Publishing Company.

Printed in the United States of America,
North Mankato, Minnesota
052013
112013

 THIS BOOK CONTAINS AT LEAST 10% RECYCLED MATERIALS.

Editor: Rebecca Felix
Series Designer: Becky Daum

Photo credits: Veronique de Viguerie/Getty Images, cover, 2, 22, 44, 49, 54; EPA European Pressphoto Agency B.V./Alamy, 6, 25, 34, 42, 47, 95; Rashid Mahmood/ AFP/Getty Images, 9; Mohammad Rehman/AFP/Getty Images, 12; iStockphoto/ Thinkstock, 14; Robert Nickelsberg/Time & Life Pictures/Getty Images, 18; Asif Hassan/AFP/Getty Images, 26; K.M. Chaudary/AP Images, 33; Abdullah Khan/AP Images, 41; Greg Baker/AP Images, 58; B.K. Bangash/AP Images, 61; Anthony Behar/ Sipa USA/AP Images, 66; Inter Services Public Relations Department/AP Images, 69; Arif Ali/AFP/Getty Images, 74, 80; Aamir Qureshi/AFP/Getty Images, 76; Queen Elizabeth Hospital/AP Images, 82; Queen Elizabeth Hospital Birmingham/Getty Images, 86

Library of Congress Control Number: 2013933057

Cataloging-in-Publication Data

Rowell, Rebecca.
 Malala Yousafzai : education activist / Rebecca Rowell.
  p. cm. -- (Essential lives)
ISBN 978-1-61783-897-2
Includes bibliographical references and index.
1. Yousafzai, Malala, 1997- --Juvenile literature. 2. Youth--Political activity--Pakistan--Biography--Juvenile literature. 3. Social justice--Pakistan--Biography--Juvenile literature. 4. Social justice--Study and teaching--Juvenile literature. I. Title.
370/.92--dc23
[B]   2013933057

CONTENTS

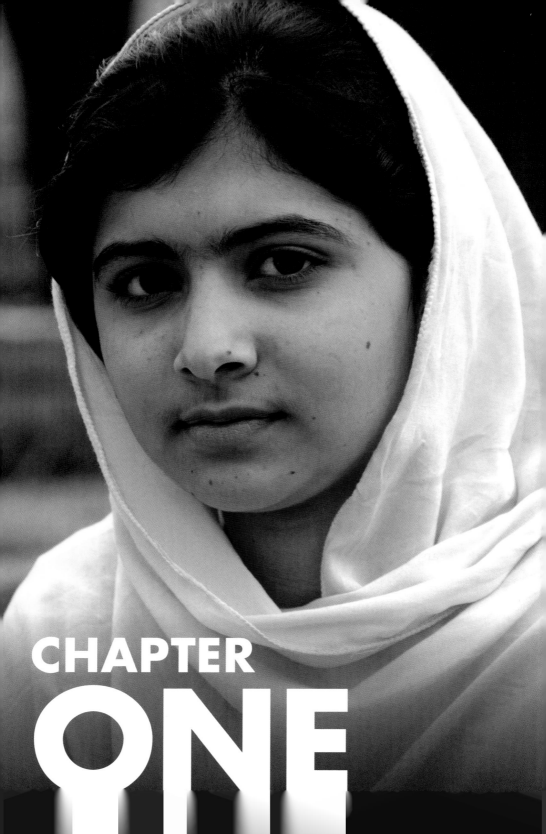

CHAPTER
ONE

ASSASSINATION ATTEMPT

The vehicle traveled along the road, taking its cargo of students home on Tuesday, October 9, 2012, just as it did every other day after school. Malala Yousafzai was one of the 25 passengers onboard from the all-girl Khushal Public School. Malala's school was in Mingora, which is the main city in Swat Valley, the area in the northwest Pakistani province of Khyber Pakhtunkhwa where the Pashtun teenager and her family lived. When morning classes finished that Tuesday, Malala boarded the vehicle as usual. She sat next to her best friend. The two joked and laughed. The day seemed like any other for the 15-year-old Pakistani girl. Khushal school was one of her favorite places to be. Malala's father was a teacher there and also ran the school. Malala learned from him the importance of education, and she dreamed of becoming a politician.

Pakistani teenager Malala Yousafzai is passionate about education and making it accessible to girls in her country.

Malala's usual, happy routine of commuting to and from school changed quickly and dramatically that day. Malala would not make it home.

Singled Out

As the vehicle continued on its route, a man halted it by waving down the driver. The stranger asked if the bus had come from Khushal Public School. As the driver responded, a second man walked around outside the vehicle and then climbed onboard. The schoolchildren initially thought the man was boarding their bus as a joke. They soon found out it was not. The man was on a mission. He asked, "Where's Malala, who is Malala?"[1] As the one Muslim girl onboard who did not cover her face, Malala stood out. Still, she responded to the gunman's questions: "I'm Malala."[2]

Pakistani police examine the site of Malala's attack: the vehicle in which she rode to and from school in Mingora.

The gunman promptly shot the teenager. "He opened fire and with one bullet she was down," recalled Kainat Riaz, a friend and classmate who was on the bus.[3] Malala appeared dead, but she was just badly injured. Kainat was also shot, as was another of Malala's friends.

In moments, the children were in chaos. "Everyone was screaming. People started crying," Kainat said.[4] Realizing what had happened, the driver sped off, and the gunmen got away.

Why Malala?

Young Malala had made a name for herself in Pakistan and beyond as an activist. Since age 11, she had been vocal about education and her rights. She made it clear she wanted an education and was an activist for education for all girls in her country. Her words defied the Taliban, an oppressive religious and political group that ruled by militant force where Malala lived. The religion of Islam affects all who live in Pakistan—even

EMPOWERING WOMEN: A GLOBAL PRIORITY

Equality—in education and life in general—is difficult for women to achieve in Pakistan and many other countries. Organizations worldwide are fighting this issue and a variety of other global issues through eight Millennium Development Goals established by the United Nations (UN) in September 2000. The goals focus on reducing poverty, hunger, child mortality, and diseases, as well as improving primary education, gender equality, maternal health, environmental sustainability, and global partnerships.

Two goals in particular reflect Malala's ideals and message: the first is achieving universal primary education. The second is promoting gender equality and empowering women. Educating girls reaches far beyond the individual students. Educated women can educate their children. An African proverb notes, "If you educate a man you educate an individual, but if you educate a woman you educate a nation."[5]

the minute minority who do not follow Islam. This is in part due to terrorist groups, such as the Taliban, that have extreme Islamic views and try to force them on others. The Taliban in Pakistan believes girls should not be educated. Because Malala loved school and believed all girls, including herself, have a right to attend school, the Taliban opposed her.

The Taliban held great power in Swat Valley. As a female living under such rule, it was difficult for Malala to get the education she wanted. The Taliban had banned girls from attending school at least once before. For a time in 2009, the Taliban completely closed Malala's school. They had made the Swat district a dangerous place to live.

At one point, Malala, her mother, and her two brothers had left their father, friends, and village. Similar to many other residents of Swat, they went into exile to stay safe and alive. Malala's father, Ziauddin, also left Swat for a time. But because the family believed he was a Taliban target, he went elsewhere while his family stayed with different family members in other parts of the country, waiting for the day they could return home and live safely.

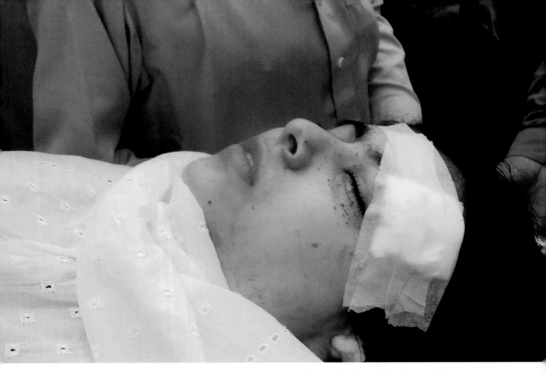

Malala survived being shot in the head by the Taliban, but her fight for recovery was just beginning.

The family survived the separation and happily reunited after a few months. Malala, excited to return home to her schoolbooks, eventually went back to her classes. Khushal Public School reopened, and Malala got back to studying. She continued speaking out in support of education. This behavior enraged the Taliban. The group decided to kill Malala because she advocated "Western thinking."[6]

Uncertain Future

The fact the Taliban was threatened by the words and ideas of a child and sought to kill her speaks to the organization's ethics. It also says a great deal about Malala. She did not let their words and actions deter her or her mission.

Documentary filmmaker Samar Minallah has worked with Malala's people, the Pashtuns. After the attack, she said of Malala, "She symbolizes the brave girls of Swat. She knew her voice was important, so she spoke up for the rights of children. Even adults didn't have a vision like hers."[7]

The assassination attempt brought greater attention to the young activist and her mission as word of the attack spread the globe via newspapers, television, and Web sites. The gunman's bullet had struck Malala in the head, passed through her neck, and lodged above her shoulder. She was in critical condition in a hospital. The Taliban had failed—she was alive, at least for now.

PASHTUN

Malala is Pashtun. The Pashtun are an ethnic group of people that live between northeastern Afghanistan and along the Indus River in northern Pakistan. Pashtun people make up a larger portion of Afghanistan's population than Pakistan's population. Though the exact origins of the Pashtun are unclear, according to folklore, the people are related to King Saul of Israel, descending from his grandson Afghana.

The Pashtun people speak Pashto, which is sometimes called Afghani and is an official language of Afghanistan. Pashto is also spoken in India, Iran, and Tajikistan.

CHAPTER
TWO

PAKISTAN

Located in southern Asia, Malala's homeland has a varied landscape and people. Although Pakistan has existed as a nation for only a short time, its history is long, with inhabitants dating back thousands of years. Religion has played an important role in Pakistan for centuries and continues to do so today. Political upheaval, economic strife, terrorist attacks, and natural disasters are common. Together, these factors shape Pakistani society and people, including Malala.

History

One of the earliest known civilizations settled along Pakistan's Indus River thousands of years ago. The Indus Valley Civilization was established in what is now Pakistan in approximately 2600 BCE. Throughout the centuries, many other groups moved into the region. They included, in order, the Persians, Greeks, Huns, Arabs, Mongols, Mughals, and British.

Pakistan has a varied landscape and a long history.

Some of the groups who occupied Pakistan made lasting changes that are visible today. Arabs introduced Islam to the region. The British influence was broad, affecting language, laws, architecture, sports, and more.

Initially, Pakistan existed in two parts: East and West. Part of India separated the two areas. Since the division, Pakistan and India have battled in multiple wars. The first two, fought from 1947 to 1948 and in 1965, were over control of Kashmir, an area northeast of Pakistan and northwest of India. These wars have not resolved the issue of Kashmir. Today, the region is divided in two, with Pakistan overseeing one part and India the other. A third war, in 1971, changed Pakistan geographically when East Pakistan became its own nation, Bangladesh.

NAMING PAKISTAN

The name Pakistan is a combination of the names of five provinces that were part of British-occupied India. The *P*, *A*, *K*, and *I* come from Punjab, Afghania, Kashmir, and Indus-Sind, while *stan* is taken from Balochistan. In the Urdu language, Pakistan can mean "land of the pure."[1]

Government and Politics: Changing Leadership

Pakistan's unsteady leadership has shifted several times between civil and military control. Its government is a federal republic with three branches: executive, legislative, and judicial. The president is the head of the country. The prime minister is the head of government institutions.

From 1947 to 1958, Pakistan had a democratic government. Successive coups in 1958 launched the country's first period of military rule, which lasted until 1971. A second democracy, led by Zulfikar Ali Bhutto, ruled from 1971 to 1977. Bhutto's military head of staff, General Mohammad Zia-ul-Haq, staged a coup in 1977. This started a second period of military control, which lasted until 1988. During this time, in 1979, Zia tried to make Pakistan an Islamic state through such measures as implementing Islamic law, and the government executed Bhutto. A new period of democracy began after Zia died in a plane crash in August 1988.

First Female Prime Minister

Though many Pakistani females, including Malala, often struggle today for equal rights, women have held positions of power in the past. Pakistanis made history in 1988 by electing Benazir Bhutto, the daughter of ousted president Bhutto, as prime minister. Benazir was the Muslim world's first female leader. This was no small feat in male-dominated Pakistan. Benazir lived

Benazir Bhutto rose to power as Pakistan's prime minister in the late 1980s, despite the country's political history of excluding women.

Malala's dream of getting an education, having studied at the prestigious Harvard and Oxford Universities. Benazir spoke with strength and conviction, setting the stage for other strong female Pakistani voices, including Malala's. However, Benazir's path was often difficult. Her struggles included exile, house arrest, imprisonment, and accusations of corruption. The last of these led to her dismissal as prime minister in 1990. She held the position again from 1993 to 1996.

After her party lost elections in 1997 and Benazir faced legal troubles, she left the country in 1999. Pakistani laws kept Benazir from seeking a third term as prime minister and barred her from holding an office for her party. Arrest warrants kept Benazir out of Pakistan for eight years. She returned in October 2007 after the president, Pervez Musharraf, granted her amnesty. But Benazir's future role in Pakistan was yet to be determined—and it never would be. Assassins killed Benazir on December 27, 2007, shooting her and exploding a bomb near her vehicle during a motorcade procession at an election rally.

Pakistan was under its third period of military rule while Benazir was in exile, lasting from 1999 to 2008. In 2008, a new democratic era began when Pakistanis chose Yousuf Raza Gilani as prime minister and elected a new president: Benazir's widower, Asif Ali Zardari.

Deadly Forces

In addition to dealing with a government that seems to be in constant flux, Pakistanis have faced deadly forces—some human, some natural. The Taliban, a militant group that took power in Afghanistan in 1996, expanded in Pakistan and fought for control. The group used threats and violence to take hold in areas such as Swat Valley, where Malala lives. The group was responsible for the attack on Benazir, and later, on Malala.

The nation has faced natural disasters, too. Earthquakes and floods have caused tremendous damage to personal property, farms, and infrastructure across the country, including in Malala's Swat Valley, as recently as 2010.

THE 2010 FLOODS

In 2010, Pakistan had the worst flooding in its history. Record rainfall in the northwest, where Malala is from, began around July 22 and caused flash floods in multiple provinces. By August 1, the flooding, which included the Indus River, had killed an estimated 1,000 people and forced at least 1 million more from their homes.[2] The rushing water moved south as rain continued in the northwest. By the middle of August, 20 percent of Pakistan was struggling with rising water levels.[3]

Problems surrounding the flooding lasted for months. By October, the Indus water levels were mostly back to normal. But even after the water subsided, hundreds of thousands of flood victims continued to live in makeshift camps with poor sanitation and not enough food.

The floods destroyed millions of acres of crops and killed many livestock. The water also damaged or destroyed hundreds of medical facilities and thousands of schools, in addition to washing away thousands of miles of road and railway.

Pakistan's government estimated the economic loss from damage caused by the flooding at $43 billion.[4] Donations from a variety of sources totaled $1.3 billion—just a fraction of damage estimates.[5] Many Pakistanis wondered how they would survive. In early 2013, many who suffered from the devastation still continued struggling, but several groups, such as International Medical Corps, offered aid.

People

Pakistan has more than 190 million inhabitants.[6] Pakistanis belong to several ethnic groups. Most of them—almost 45 percent—are Punjabi. Malala's people, the Pashtun, are the second-largest group, making up a little more than 15 percent of the population. Other smaller groups include the Sindhi, Saraiki, Muhajir, and Balochi.[7]

The nation's population is young. Most Pakistanis are 54 years old or younger. The median age is approximately 22 years. Malala is part of the abundant youth majority in Pakistan: 56 percent of people are under the age of 35.[8]

Most Pakistanis live in rural areas. Approximately one-third of the population, including Malala, is urban. Bordering the Arabian Sea in the south, Karachi is the most-populated city in Pakistan, with more than 13 million inhabitants.[9] Mingora, Malala's hometown, is the largest city in Swat district. Recent estimates place the population near 500,000.[10]

More than one-fifth of the Pakistani population lives below the poverty line.[11] Most poor Pakistanis—80 percent—live in rural areas.[12] Poverty in Pakistan

Malala is a part of Pakistan's majority as a youth and Muslim but a part of the minority as a literate, Pashtun female.

is due to several causes. Agriculture is the core of rural economies. People living in mountainous areas struggle to find quality land to farm, while those living in drier areas have a limited supply of water. In other areas, people simply do not have much land to farm. A small number of landowners hold most of the land throughout Pakistan. This leaves a limited amount of land for millions of others to own.

Poor or limited education can also lead to and worsen poverty. A little more than half of Pakistanis are literate. Males have a higher literacy rate than females. Approximately 69 percent of men can read and write, while the percentage for women is approximately 40 percent.[13] This makes Malala part of a minority and shows why her advocacy for education is so needed, especially for herself and other girls.

Pakistanis speak a variety of languages. Urdu is the official language, but it is used by only 8 percent of Pakistanis. Approximately half—48 percent —of Pakistanis speak Punjabi.[14] Pakistanis also speak English, which is an official language; Sindhi; Saraiki; Urdu; and Pashto, which Malala speaks; among other languages.

Malala is a part of the more than 96 percent of Pakistan's population that are Muslim, meaning they follow the Islam religion.[15] The remaining

HEALTH RISKS IN PAKISTAN

Pakistanis are at a high risk for contracting several infectious diseases. Many factors contribute to the problem, including contaminated water, overcrowding, lack of sanitation, and the general state of simply living in a poor society. In addition, vaccination and health knowledge is limited. Diseases that can be acquired through food and water include bacterial diarrhea, hepatitis A and E, and typhoid fever. Malaria and dengue fever are possible, too, traveling from person to person via hosts such as mosquitoes. Polio and measles are also prevalent in Pakistan.

population practices other religions, including Christianity and Hinduism.

Pakistan has a patriarchal society. Males are the major decision makers, land and business owners, and heads of government, family, and religion. In addition to being male-dominated, Pakistani social life is steeped in religious tradition. Society reflects Islamic tradition, which has rules for all aspects of life.

Fighting for Females

Pakistani women are far from being equal to men in nearly all aspects of society. However, in addition to Malala's education advocacy, many Pakistani women have fought for equality. Some have done so with help from or as part of more than a dozen women's rights groups in Pakistan.

Even with such groups, the challenges are great. Women in Pakistan face violence in many forms, including disfiguring acid attacks, murder, mutilation, and rape.

Women who are activists face even greater risks. Groups such as the Taliban often threaten female activists in Pakistan or attack them, as they did Malala. Many activists point out the government's failure

Supporters of liberal Pakistani political party the Muttahida Qaumi Movement, which believes in female equality, rally for Malala.

to support women's rights, especially in defending female activists against harm. Some place equal blame on Pakistan's government as the militant attackers because officials do not often provide protection against such violence.

To support and empower women, officials must contend with strong adversaries, such as the Taliban. This is an ongoing challenge as the terrorist group continues to violently enforce its extreme Islamic views on the nation and its people.

CHAPTER
THREE

ISLAM

Islam plays a central role in the lives of the people of Pakistan. Most Pakistanis are Muslim, but Islam's influence impacts even those who are not. The religion's importance is evident in the nation's official name: the Islamic Republic of Pakistan. Islam shaped the history of the region and continues to influence Pakistan's culture today.

History of Islam

Islam is centuries old. It was founded by the Prophet Muhammad in the 600s. Muhammad was born in approximately 570 in Mecca, a city in present-day Saudi Arabia. As an adult, Muhammad often spent time in seclusion, meditating and praying. He would spend nights on Mount Hira, located north of Mecca, thinking about his city and the problems of society. During one of these times of solitude, when Muhammad was approximately 40 years old, an angel who resembled a man appeared and spoke to him:

Hands upheld in Islamic style, Pakistani schoolchildren pray for Malala's recovery after her attack.

Recite in the name of thy lord who created, Created man from a clot; Recite in the name of thy lord, Who taught by the pen, Taught man what he knew not.[1]

Muhammad thought he was being attacked by an evil force and ran away. The angel called after him: "O Muhammad, you are the messenger of God, and I am the angel Gabriel."[2] This was the first revelation by God to Muhammad. More messages followed for 23 years, until Gabriel finally told Muhammad to share God's message with others.

MECCA

Mecca is the center of Islam. It is the birthplace of Muhammad, the religion's founder. Mecca is located in western Saudi Arabia, not far from the Red Sea. It has a population of almost 1.3 million people.[3] The city is so sacred only Muslims are allowed within its boundaries.

Mecca is home to several Muslim shrines. The Ka'bah is the holiest. This shrine is near the center of the Haram Mosque, or the Great Mosque, which is the focus of activity in the city. When Muslims pray, no matter how far away, they always face Mecca. Most Muslims attempt a hajj, or pilgrimage, to the city at least once in their lives.

Millions of Muslims visit the Great Mosque each year. The mosque began as a wall in 638. The structure grew and changed over the centuries. The most recent renovation was completed in 1984, increasing the size to approximately 3.84 million square feet (356,700 sq m). Builders installed escalators, passageways, and tunnels to improve pedestrian traffic for the 820,000 Muslims the mosque can hold.[4]

Muhammad did as the angel commanded and shared the message. At the time, Meccans believed in many gods, so some people did not like what Muhammad said. Others were interested in his message and became his followers. In 622, local rulers ran Muhammad and his followers out of Mecca. Muhammad and his people left and lived in an oasis named Yathrib, which became Medina.

Muhammad and his followers survived in Medina by raiding and fighting. They attacked caravans passing through from Mecca. In 628, Muhammad and the Meccans signed a truce to end the attacks. The next year, when one of his followers was murdered, presumably by a Meccan or Meccan supporter, Muhammad led his people in attacking and defeating the Meccans. This win increased Muhammad's reputation and importance.

Muhammad died in 632 from illness, but his followers continued to spread his word, the word of Islam, which means "submission" in Arabic.[5] It can also mean "surrender."[6] Within 100 years of Muhammad's death, Islam had spread from Spain to India. It would continue to expand throughout the centuries. Today, Islam is a major world religion, with more than 1 billion

practicing Muslims.[7] There are two major sects of
Islam: Sunni and Shi'ite. Malala and her family are
Sunni Muslims.

SUNNI AND SHI'ITE

Islam has two branches: Sunni and Shi'ite. Sunnis, such as Malala and her family, believe Muhammad's successors may be elected, while Shi'ites believe only direct descendants of Muhammad can hold such authority. Most Muslims worldwide are Sunni. In Pakistan, 85 to 90 percent of Muslims are Sunni and 10 to 15 percent are Shi'ite.[9]

Allah and the Five Pillars

Muslims believe in a single, all-powerful God. This God is the same one of Judaism and Christianity. Muslims refer to God as Allah.

Unlike other religions, Islam does not have ministers or other clergy. Muslims worship God directly, not through appointed religious representatives.

Muslims have five responsibilities known as the Five Pillars of Islam. They are: belief, worship, fasting, almsgiving, and pilgrimage. These pillars guide Muslims' lives.

For the first pillar, a Muslim must state in Arabic his or her belief. The person must say, "There is no god but God and that Muhammad is His messenger."[8] For worship, Muslims pray five times a day: dawn, noon, mid-afternoon, sunset, and at nightfall. The third pillar is fasting. From sunrise to sunset during the month of Ramadan, Muslims are not to eat, drink, smoke, or have sex. Islam stresses helping the poor, which is referred to as almsgiving. Each year, Muslims are expected to donate a certain portion of their belongings to the poor. If able, each Muslim should travel to Mecca during the beginning of the twelfth month of the Muslim calendar at least once in his or her life to complete the fifth pillar. Known as hajj, the pilgrimage includes wearing special attire and participating in specific ceremonies.

The Koran and Sharia

The Koran is the Islamic holy book. It has 114 chapters and contains Muhammad's message to the world. That message came to Muhammad from God, so Muslims consider the book God's word.

Similar to other religions, Islam has rules its believers are to follow. Islamic law is called Sharia, and it addresses all areas of life for Muslims, including business, family, and politics. Sharia comes from multiple sources. The main two are the Koran and Muhammad's example, which is found in what he said, did, and taught. Traditional guides to Sharia usually have four parts, each focusing on a different area of law: commercial dealings, marriage and divorce, penal, and personal acts of worship.

According to Sharia, all behaviors fit into one of five categories: obligatory, recommended, permissible, disliked, or forbidden. Most behaviors are considered permissible.

Muslim Women

As a Pakistani Muslim, Malala has experienced gender discrimination. Many Muslim women are not treated equally to men. Many people believe Muslim women are mistreated due to Islamic rules. However, what appears to be oppression from Islam is actually the result of local culture.

Islam grants Muslim women many rights. The Koran specifies several. Women may deny a possible husband, divorce in specific situations, and inherit

WEARING A VEIL

Muslim women often wear some type of veil. These veils can range from a scarf that covers their hair to a full-length burka, a loose piece of clothing that covers the entire body and face. The Koran decrees both sexes must dress modestly, but how much of her body a Muslim woman covers up usually reflects her social status, not religion. Historically, wealthier women tend to cover themselves more than poor or rural women.

The Taliban cites strict belief in Islam, but most Pakistanis believe the group's interpretation of Sharia is extreme.

and own property. In addition, it is prohibited to kill a baby because she is female, and Muslims are expected to educate both girls and boys. This means, in accordance with Islam and contrary to the Taliban's orders, Malala and all other Pakistani girls should indeed attend school and receive an education.

We Conde
brutal atta
Taliban
MALALA YOU

CHAPTER FOUR

THE TALIBAN

When the Taliban made news in October 2012 for attempting to kill Malala, it was not the first time the group had been the subject of headlines. Afghanistan's Taliban had been causing upheaval in the region for more than a decade. The group's offshoot in Pakistan, the perpetrators of the assault on Malala and her classmates, had been terrorizing Pakistan for several years.

Birth of a Terrorist Group

The Soviet Union invaded Afghanistan in 1979. Millions of Afghans fled in response, escaping across the border to Pakistan. A decade later, Afghanistan was struggling with great civil disorder as troops from the Soviet Union departed and communist rule ended. Young people formed the Taliban in 1994 to help create order. Most of them were students who had trained in Islamic religious schools created in the 1980s in northern Pakistan for

Pakistanis protest the Taliban's attack on Malala. The Taliban has become known worldwide for its acts of violence against people such as Malala who resist its oppressive rules.

Afghani refugees. The word Taliban means "students" in Pashto.[1]

In 1994, the Taliban helped to establish order in southern Afghanistan by overtaking the warlords who controlled the area. By the end of 1996, the Taliban had taken Kabul, Afghanistan's capital. They did so with support from the Pashtuns in the south. Conservative Islamic groups from beyond the nation's borders also supported the Taliban.

JOURNALISTS IN DANGER

Because of Taliban terrorism, Pakistan is not a safe place for journalists. The Committee to Protect Journalists has noted Pakistan is "one of the deadliest nations in the world for the press."[2] The organization said that since 1992, murderers have taken the lives of more than 50 journalists in Pakistan, and the government has not arrested the attackers.[3]

On January 17, 2012, two gunmen shot Mukarram Khan Aatif near Peshawar in the Swat district. Aatif worked for a television station and for a radio station that was part of the US station Voice of America. A Taliban spokesman said the Taliban had cautioned Aatif "a number of times to stop anti-Taliban reporting, but he didn't do so. He finally met his fate."[4]

Malik Mumtaz worked for the Pakistani newspaper News International and for Geo, a television network. Mumtaz was shot heading home after a funeral on February 27, 2013, in the northwestern part of Pakistan. On March 1, reporter Mahmud Afridi was gunned down by people on a motorcycle in a southwestern district. Afridi worked for a local newspaper and was president of a press club. No person or group claimed responsibility for the deaths of Mumtaz and Afridi.

Non-Pashtun groups in other parts of Afghanistan resisted the Pashtun-dominant Taliban. Afghanistan was mostly Pashtun and such groups did not want the new Taliban organization to continue the Pashtun control over minorities. Their fighting was futile. By 2001, the Taliban controlled most of the country. From there, the Taliban's control grew, along with its extremist ideals and violent and controlling behavior.

Challenging Practices

Many people worldwide do not agree with Taliban views, especially their views of women. The group essentially keeps women from public life, in accordance with their view of Islam. Women are not supposed to attend school or work outside the home. The group believes in harsh punishments—sometimes in the form of an attack, as was Malala's case— for those who defy these rules. In addition to enforcing strict ideals, the Taliban has created much destruction, systematically ruining artifacts that are not Islamic. In 2001, ignoring requests from across the globe, the group destroyed two enormous historic Buddha statues in Bamiyan, Afghanistan, located approximately 80 miles (130 km) northwest of Kabul.

The seeds of the Taliban's downfall were sown when it allowed other militant Islamic groups to hide out in Afghanistan. Chief among them was Osama bin Laden, the leader of the terrorist group al-Qaeda.

The United States wanted bin Laden to pay for his role in the September 2001 attacks in the United States. The Taliban refused to hand over the terrorist leader. The United States responded with military power and toppled Taliban control in Afghanistan. But the Taliban was not wiped out. Rebels continued to challenge US forces and their allies. The rebel groups also expanded, with some establishing power—at least intermittently—in neighboring Pakistan.

The Taliban in Pakistan

The Pakistani Taliban is a militant organization. Most of Pakistan's Taliban are part of one group. This Pakistani Taliban's official name is the Tehrik-i-Taliban Pakistan. It is not the only militant group in the country, but it has more members and power than other groups. The Pakistani Taliban is its own group, separate from the Afghani Taliban, but it is similar in its extreme views of religion.

Taliban leaders in Pakistan founded their branch during a secret gathering on December 13, 2007. They formed their group to present a united front. They wanted to bring together their resources, including people, to fight Pakistan's government forces. They also wanted to aid the Afghani Taliban in fighting US troops and US allies on the International Security Assistance Force. However, the Pakistani Taliban could not spare many members to fight in Afghanistan because it was busy fighting military forces in Pakistan.

When the Pakistani Taliban formed, Baitullah Mehsud became its leader. He oversaw the group until August 2009, when the US killed him in an attack by unmanned aerial combat vehicles commonly called drones. Following Mehsud's death, the sect split into multiple groups. The splintering did not stop the Pakistani Taliban's attacks.

Reign of Terror

The Pakistani Taliban uses violence to fight for two goals. In addition to its original objective of pushing the United States out of the region, the group wants to take down Pakistan's current government and institute Islamic Sharia rule. The Pakistani Taliban opposes the nation's constitution and its democratic process.

To achieve its goal of establishing an Islamic state in place of the current Pakistani state, the Taliban targets members of Pakistan's military and government. The group

Pakistan's government and military, seen patrolling
Swat in 2009, continuously struggle to keep the Taliban
in check, and often fail to do so efficiently.

41

Armed Pakistani Taliban patrol near Swat Valley, where they have caused terror and displaced its residents.

focuses on civilians, too. Often, the method of attack is suicide bomb, and places of worship are not exempt. On April 1, 2011, more than 40 people died at a Sufi shrine in the Punjab district.[5] The Pakistani Taliban openly admitted it set off the two suicide bombs that caused the destruction.

The group's extreme beliefs and violent acts have caused chaos and incredible harm in Pakistan. Members' actions have created uncertainty in the lives of many, including those in Malala's hometown region of Swat, where Taliban rule is present. The organization's terrorism was so threatening it often interrupted the lives of many people who lived in northwest Pakistan. Many residents escaped, looking for places safer than their own villages or districts. Those seeking exile included the residents of Mingora, Malala's birthplace.

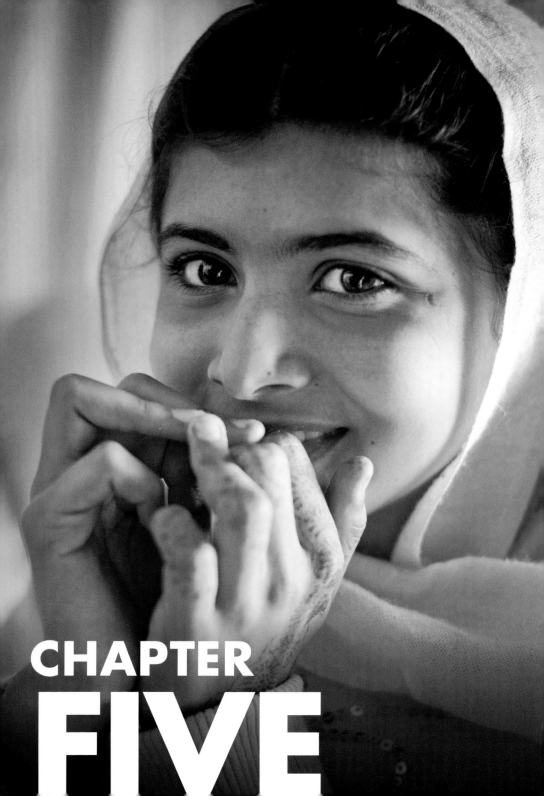

CHAPTER
FIVE

BIRTH OF AN ACTIVIST

Malala Yousafzai was born on July 12, 1997, in Mingora, located in the Swat district of northwestern Pakistan. Malala is the oldest of Ziauddin and Toorpekai's three children. She has two brothers: Khushal and Atal.

Malala's parents are Pashtun. The couple named Malala after Malalai Joya, a Pashtun folk heroine who battled British troops during the Anglo-Afghan War in 1880. Shortly after Malala was born, her father added her name to family records. This was not common in Pakistan's patriarchal society, where sons are valued more than daughters.

A Father's Lesson

Malala was born into a lower-middle-class family. Although she did not grow up with a great deal of money, she had a wealth of support. Ziauddin is strong,

The only daughter in her family, Malala has been treated with fairness and equality since birth.

thoughtful, and educated, and he valued and encouraged his daughter.

Ziauddin is a teacher. He founded Khushal Public School, the school Malala attended in Mingora. Mustafa Qadri is a Pakistan researcher at Amnesty International, a humanitarian organization. Qadri knows Malala's father well. He described him:

> *Her father has a sort of revolutionary commitment to his cause. He is an incredibly unique and complex person.*

GROWING UP IN SWAT VALLEY

Swat, the northwestern Pakistani district where Malala was born and raised, is similar in size to the state of Delaware. More than 1 million people live in Swat Valley within the district.[1] The huge district has many large cities, including Malala's birthplace and hometown of Mingora. The district's urban cities are surrounded by the region's natural beauty, which has attracted many wealthy Pakistanis and tourists. The region has abundant vegetation. Its beautiful forests, majestic waterways, and picturesque mountains and valleys earned Swat Valley the nickname "Switzerland of Pakistan" because of its resemblance to the beautiful European country.[2]

Malala's town lies on the Swat River, which runs through the valley, fed with water from melting snow and glaciers. The river is important for farming. Canals carry water from Swat River to fields of crops consisting of mainly sugarcane and wheat.

In addition to offering a beautiful landscape, the district where Malala grew up has several cultural offerings as well. Swat has many historical Buddhist sites, from a time when people of that religion dwelled in the area. Today, Swat visitors can see a variety of ruins, including caves, inscriptions, monasteries, rock carvings, and stupas, a type of Buddhist shrine.

Malala's ideals and passion for equality and education have been shaped and supported by her father, Ziauddin.

> He's a deeply religious man, in the best sense of the term. I remember him constantly talking about his Islam and that it tells him to get his daughter educated and to make sure that women get the same rights as men.[3]

Qadri also said Ziauddin "is very brave, very eloquent, as is Malala."[4]

Defying the Taliban

Malala and Ziauddin's bravery was apparent as the Taliban's power in Swat grew in 2007 and turned into terrorist attacks in 2008. In July 2008, the Taliban launched a series of attacks, bombing government bodies, including schools. The group focused on girls' schools, citing the institutions' defiance of Islam. Attackers ruined hundreds of buildings and threatened teachers and students. Ziauddin kept his daughter's school open, but doing so was very risky. The Taliban could attack it or him at any time.

That fall, Ziauddin went to Peshawar, the capital of their province, to attend a protest against the Taliban's campaign against girls' schools. The event was held at Peshawar's press club and included members of the national press. Ziauddin did not go to the event alone. He brought 11-year-old Malala. On September 1, the young student gave a speech: "How Dare the Taliban Take Away My Basic Right to an Education." It was her first public appearance. Many people liked what Malala said, but her words also brought negative attention from Taliban members.

Blogging anonymously about her daily life under Taliban control, Malala reached a wider audience with her message of support for equal education for Pakistani girls.

The Secret Blogger

In January 2009, Taliban militants issued a declaration via radio: "From January 15, girls will not be allowed to attend schools."[5] The militants issued the edict because they believed educating females went against Islam rule.

That same month, Abdul Hai Kakar, a news correspondent on behalf of major worldwide news agency the British Broadcasting Corporation (BBC) in Peshawar, asked Ziauddin if one of his students would write about life in Swat under Taliban control. A girl volunteered, but her parents were afraid of the repercussions and would not let her take on the project. Malala agreed to do it instead. To provide readers with a personal, realistic view of what was going in the Swat district, Malala shared experiences from her daily life with the world via the Internet. She kept a diary, recording her experiences living with fighting between the Taliban and military forces. Malala spoke with Kakar weekly, dictating to him what she wrote. The BBC published Malala's diary entries in a newspaper and online at the BBC's Urdu Web site, a version of the company's site in the Urdu language. Malala wrote under the pen name Gul Makai for anonymity.

The BBC also published Malala's writings in English, calling them *Diary of a Pakistani Schoolgirl*. The BBC published entries from January to March. The first entry appeared on January 3. Titled "I Am Afraid," Malala explains how the Taliban's announcement of the upcoming ban on girls in school had affected attendance:

> I had a terrible dream yesterday with military helicopters and the Taleban. I have had such dreams since the launch of the military operation in Swat. . . . I was afraid going to school because the Taleban had issued an edict banning all girls from attending schools.

Only 11 students attended the class out of 27. The number decreased because of Taleban's edict. My three friends have shifted to Peshawar, Lahore, and Rawalpindi with their families after this edict.[6]

Malala also wrote about overhearing her father discuss three bodies that were found. She described how the dangerous environment of the Swat Valley interfered with her family's activities, such as going on picnics on Sundays.

Mention of the Taliban returns in Malala's January 5 entry. In it, she describes dressing differently than usual for school. Her principal told the students to not wear their uniforms, perhaps to make it less obvious they were attending school. Instead, the girls were to wear "normal clothes."[7] Malala wore a favorite dress. It was pink. Her classmates wore colorful dresses, too. During morning assembly, the girls were told another rule: they were not to wear colorful clothes, as the Taliban does not like girls in

"We were absolutely thrilled by the way she was writing. I wouldn't call it mature. I would call it a very, very fresh, untainted and straight-from-the-heart sort of a take on what was going on. She would use these little anecdotal bits to bring out the atmosphere of fear surrounding schools and children in particular. She was clearly a very, very intelligent and a very observant girl."[8]
—*Aamer Ahmed Khan, head of BBC's Urdu service, on Malala's writing*

eye-catching clothing. The girls' pretty outfits put them at risk of attack.

In another entry, Malala writes about the possibility of not returning to school because the Taliban was closing girls' schools in accordance with their Islamic beliefs. The thought did not make Malala happy:

> I was in a bad mood while going to school because winter vacations are starting from tomorrow. The principal announced the vacations but did not mention the date the school was to reopen. This was the first time this has happened. . . . I am of the view that the school will one day reopen but while leaving I looked at the building as if I would not come here again.[9]

Malala's Television Interview

February 2009 brought young Malala more attention. That month, a cease-fire between the Pakistani military and the Taliban was possible. The Taliban would agree only if the government instituted its extreme version of Sharia law. Malala attended a protest against the Taliban and met Hamid Mir, a popular television journalist. He interviewed her on his show, which was known for being anti-Taliban. Malala said to Mir in the interview, "All I want is an education. And I am afraid of no one."[11]

Malala was firm in her stance, certain of herself and her message. But soon, the Pakistani Taliban would make life in Swat even more difficult. A reporter was filming the troubles in Swat, the closing of Khushal Public School, and Malala's experience as she escaped the valley for safer surroundings.

"I have the right to play. I have the right to sing. I have the right to talk. I have the right to go to market. I have the right to speak up."[12]
—Malala Yousafzai, CNN interview, 2011

CHAPTER
SIX

EXILE, ADVANCES, AND HONORS

When Malala blogged about her experiences in Swat in 2009, she shared with the world the challenges she and others in her area faced because of the Taliban. For months, violence and death were common occurrences, as approximately 12,000 government troops and 3,000 Taliban members battled.[1] Though their numbers were only one-quarter those of the army, the Taliban seemed to be succeeding in taking control of Swat Valley. They killed several officials and police officers.

In addition to declaring all girls' schools in Swat Valley closed in January 2009, the Taliban took stronger measures to control residents, punishing people they believed were not following the strict Islamic rules the group promoted. The Taliban took punishments to the extreme. For example, the Taliban prohibited dancing

From the time she was a young girl, local Taliban terrorized Malala's town. But this did not deter Malala from her dreams or quiet her activism for educational rights.

and watching television. When caught disobeying this order, some offenders were beheaded.

In the summer of 2009, Pakistan's army retaliated against the Taliban in a large attack. In anticipation of and during this push, many of Swat's residents fled for their lives that May, including Malala.

The Documentary

Malala documented her experiences living under Taliban oppression in 2009 through her blog. Adam B. Ellick, a reporter for the *New York Times*, captured the story of Swat on film. Specifically, Ellick followed Malala and her family during that time, interviewing and filming them. Malala's mother did not appear on film for cultural reasons. He used the material to create the documentary *Class Dismissed: The Death of Female Education*.

The film is approximately 30 minutes long and begins with footage of a river, then a village with traffic crossing a bridge over the river. Ziauddin's voice speaks in a voiceover: "In the area where I live, there are some people who want to stop educating girls through guns."[2] The scene changes to men shooting guns and throwing rocks—it is the Taliban in action. Malala and her father appear next on the film. Malala speaks: "I want to get

my education and I want to become a doctor."[3] Then
she begins to cry. Malala's father expresses his hope of
a different future for his daughter. He hopes she will be
a politician:

> But I see a great potential in my daughter that she can
> do more than a doctor. She can create a society where a
> medical student will be easily able to get her doctorate
> degree.[4]

The film captures the danger
Pakistanis face regularly under
Taliban rule. Several images
show beaten and bloodied
bodies. Ellick explains in his
narrative the Taliban's order
decreeing girls are not allowed
to attend school.

The film continues to
document the family over the
next few months. At first,
Malala stays home after her
school closes, but the Taliban
continues to gain power during
that time. Months later, in
May, the school is still closed,

"Today, Swat has in the
past few years become a
heartland for Pakistan Islamic
militancy. Today, this idyllic
valley of peace is burning.
Why the peace of this valley
is destroyed? Why the
peace and innocent people
of the valley are targeted?
Why our future is targeted?
Schools are not places of
learning but places of fear
and violence. Who will solve
our problems? Who will
return our valley to peace?
I think nobody. No one.
Our dreams are shattered.
And let me say, we are
destroyed."[5]
 — *Malala's classmate,
reading an essay during a
scene in* Class Dismissed:
The Death of Female
Education

Swat residents left their homes in May 2009 to escape Taliban violence.

and the situation worsens. That month, the Pakistani military launches an offensive against the terrorists. Swat becomes a war zone. Within three hours, Malala and more than 1 million other residents leave Swat for their own safety—to stay alive.[6] People flee in a chaotic scene, leaving their belongings behind. With no place to stay in Swat and no income to support his family since Khushal Public School has closed, Ziauddin sends Malala, her mother, and her brothers to stay with family elsewhere while he goes to Peshawar.

Peshawar is the capital of the province where Swat Valley is located. It is the center of the fight against the Taliban in Pakistan. Ziauddin stays with three other men, who are also exiles, in Peshawar. Similar to Ziauddin, one of them also runs a girls' school, while another teaches at a girls' school. The men organize rallies and press conferences in Peshawar, hoping to convince the government to take more action and regain control of Swat from the Taliban.

While Ziauddin is fighting for Swat, Malala and the rest of her family move four times in two months. Many of their Swat neighbors are living in refugee camps under conditions that are less than ideal.

The men Ziauddin is staying with in Peshawar are also husbands and fathers separated from their families. They summarize the situation: "We are missing life."[7] Malala misses school most while she is away. She cannot wait to return home to her books.

The film shows Malala's family reuniting after three months of being away from Swat. Before returning home, she and other advocates meet with US ambassador Richard Holbrooke. Malala speaks directly to the ambassador, pleading for help.

Upon returning to Mingora, Ziauddin and Malala see their valley is like a ghost town. They are eager to see their home. Malala is pleased to find her books intact, but the school is in poor condition. Ziauddin's key does not work, so he must climb a wall to get inside. Furniture is piled in a room, and there is a cigarette on the floor. Some walls have holes.

Pakistani soldiers had stayed in the building. Malala is proud of her army for protecting her, but she is not happy about the way they treated her school. The army left a letter for Ziauddin, blaming him for the turmoil in Swat. When the Taliban announced in January 2009 that girls were banned from school, the group also

Award for Youth. When the nation's prime minister, Yousuf Raza Gilani, announced Malala was the winner, he also revealed that the award would be named for Malala and given yearly to a Pakistani younger than 18.

The attention Malala received for her ideas and advocacy turned a spotlight on the issues her country was facing. However, the increased awareness and acknowledgement did not sway Taliban members to her side. Instead, the group made a decision: Malala must be silenced.

CHAPTER
SEVEN

THE UNTHINKABLE HAPPENS

Malala's increased exposure in the media spread her message worldwide, adding to the anger the Taliban had built against her. The group decided to kill the outspoken teen girl. They devised a plan.

On the afternoon of Tuesday, October 9, 2012, Taliban members put their plan into action. Gunmen stopped Malala's school vehicle. One climbed onto the back of the vehicle and asked which girl was Malala. The man fired four bullets, hitting three girls, including Malala. Upon being struck, Malala slumped over. She was in terrible pain, but she was alive. The bus driver pulled away from the attackers.

Initial Treatment

The driver sped the school bus to the Saidu Sharif Medical Complex in Mingora. Doctors at the hospital

Malala's increased outspokenness and media attention as an advocate for girls' education made her a Taliban target.

UNINTENTIONAL TARGET

Adam B. Ellick, the journalist who created the documentary film featuring Malala and Ziauddin, spoke about Ziauddin's awareness of the risk of defying the Taliban. The militant group wanted him dead. To spare his family harm, Ziauddin sometimes moved around from night to night, sleeping away from his family in different places. Ellick said of Ziauddin, "We spoke so many times about death and martyrdom . . . those conversations were about him being the bull's-eye, not Malala."[1] According to Ellick, Ziauddin was heartbroken over the Taliban's attack on Malala: "One friend met [Ziauddin] for half an hour, but they didn't utter a sentence together. They just cried together for half an hour."[2]

treated Malala and her two injured classmates. One bullet struck Malala's friend Kainat, but reports differ as to exactly where on her body—her hand or arm—she had been hit. Classmate Shazia Ramazan had two wounds. The gunman shot her arm and hand.

Malala's wounds were more serious. The terrorist's bullet entered her head right above her left eye. From there, it passed along the outside of her skull, just barely skimming past her brain. Then it moved past her jawbone and down to her neck, where it stopped. The bullet ended up buried in muscle above Malala's left shoulder blade.

Had the bullet taken another path, Malala's story would have ended that day, but the attackers failed in their assassination attempt.

To make the move, Malala traveled on a special airplane. The United Arab Emirates (UAE), a nation in the Middle East, provided an air ambulance for the transfer. Pilots took the injured Malala to Abu Dhabi, the UAE's capital, and then flew to Birmingham. Upon landing, a ground ambulance transported Malala to the Queen Elizabeth Hospital.

Those aiding Malala in recovery were growing in number. A successful recovery seemed quite possible. Malala would soon learn just how much support she had, as people around the world expressed their belief in her and her cause.

SCHOOL REOPENS SHORTLY AFTER THE ATTACK

On Friday, October 12, just days after the attack, while shooting victims Malala, Shazia Ramazan, and Kainat Riaz recovered from their wounds, their school in Mingora reopened. Some of the girls' friends and classmates returned to classes, but not all. Zafar Ali Khan, a teacher at the school, said, "We have decided to open the school after two days to overcome the fear among our students that gripped them due to the attack. The number of students is low today. We have not resumed regular teaching activity, but held an assembly to pray for Malala and the other two injured girls."[6]

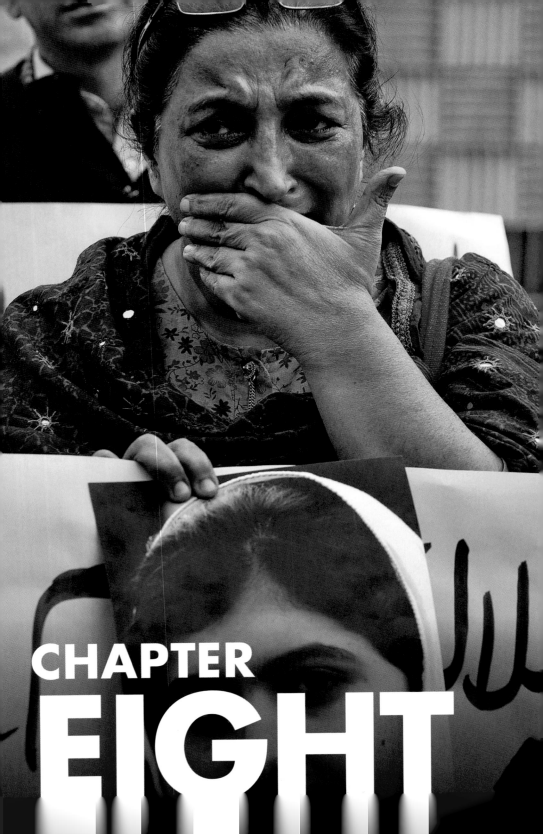

CHAPTER
EIGHT

THE WORLD RESPONDS

Pakistani supporters reacted immediately to the attack on Malala. Some gathered in small groups, holding vigils in her honor. They prayed for her recovery. In Peshawar, city officials observed a moment of silence.

As media outlets spread news of the Taliban's assassination attempt on the Pakistani teen, people near and far responded. Support for the injured girl grew as awareness of the event increased. Thousands of Malala's supporters gathered in different rallies. In Karachi, a port city in the southern part of the country, Pakistanis protested with banners and posters. Some read "Malala, our prayers are with you."[1] Others scolded the group behind the attack, reading, "Shame on you, Taliban."[2]

Pakistani human rights activist Saeeda Diep helped organize a protest in Lahore, a Pakistani city southwest of Mingora, near the Indian border, the day after

Sharing the sentiments of activists and supporters worldwide, a Pakistani protester is distraught over news of Malala's assassination attempt.

Outrage over Malala's attack spanned the globe, and protesters rallied to support Malala and her cause and condemn the Taliban's actions.

the attack. She stressed the importance of Pakistanis protesting the attack: "If they do not do this, then they should mentally prepare themselves for their own children's fate to be like Malala's."[3]

The assassination attempt united Pakistani leaders. Heads of all of Pakistan's political parties agreed the attack was wrong. This type of agreement had rarely happened before, if ever. Pakistan Foreign Minister Hina Rabbani Khar responded publicly to Malala's shooting. She was clear about what it meant for her nation:

> She has put it as a black and white question. She has put it as either you are with the future that she represents, or the future they [the Taliban] are trying to impose.[4]

Honorary Renaming

To show support for Malala, officials in Swat decided to rename Government College for Girls after the recovering teen. The decision made the school the first in the valley to be named after a female.

The school provides its 2,000 female students high school and undergraduate studies in arts and sciences.[5] Subjects are varied and include botany, chemistry, English literature, and zoology.

Local authorities wanted to send the Taliban a message by renaming the school. Kamran Rehman Khan, a local official, said, "We just want to tell them we will not be deterred by their actions."[6] Khan also explained the broader goal of the school, "We always want to send a message across the world, that here we want to develop the female gender and we also want females to come forward in society."[7]

Students at the school were afraid to attend because of the Taliban. Still, they went to classes, knowing they had a right to an education. Malala inspired them.

Seventeen-year-old Mehreen, one of the students at the renamed school, spoke about Malala:

> I think she's a very brave girl. She sacrificed her life for us, for education, that girls should take education for their bright future.[9]

Attacks Continue

The words and actions in support of Malala did not deter the Taliban. The group continued to impose threats and acts of terrorism, including attacks against girls and women. Not long after trying to kill Malala, Taliban members attacked college students riding in a van in Parachinar, in the northern part of Pakistan. The attackers threw acid at the students, striking two girls and one boy. They also shot a boy. The local Pakistani Taliban leader, Qari Muhavia, explained the Taliban's intent:

> We will never allow the girls of this area to go and get a Western education. If and when we find any girl from Parachinar going to university for an education we will target her [in] the same way, so that she might not be able to unveil her face before others.[10]

An Apology

While Muhavia spoke out on behalf of Taliban attacks, another apologized for them. On November 4, 2012, Rehana Haleem, the sister of suspect Khan responded to the attack. She said,

> Please convey a message to Malala, that I apologize for what my brother did to her. . . . What he did was intolerable. Malala is just like my sister. I'd like to express my concern for Malala on behalf of my whole family; I hope she recovers soon and returns to a happy and normal life as soon as possible. I hope Malala doesn't consider me or my family as enemies. I don't consider [Khan] my brother anymore.[11]

Malala Day and more Malala Schools

The United Nations (UN) also responded to Malala's attack. The organization declared November 10, 2012, Malala Day. Gordon Brown, former British prime minister, represented the UN in a visit to Pakistan in honor of the special day. That day, he went

INJURED CLASSMATES HONORED

The two other girls injured in the Taliban's attempted assassination of Malala were not forgotten in the aftermath of the event. Pakistan's interior minister, Rehman Malik, presented Kainat and Shazia with the Sitara-e-jurrat, which is Arabic for "star of courage."[12] It is the nation's third-highest military award and is rarely given to civilians.

A Pakistani student writes on a poster commemorating Malala Day on November 10, 2012.

to Pakistani schools, including Malala's school, spoke to educational groups and charities, and met with members of Pakistan's government, including the president.

One month after Malala was shot, her attack spurred another important announcement regarding education and schools in Pakistan. Nafisa Shah is chairwoman of the National Commission for Human Development, a nonprofit organization that aims to improve accessibility to education and health care in poor Pakistani communities. In mid-November, Shah announced that Pakistan was planning to open several new schools in Malala's name. The "Malala Schools" were slated for 16 areas around the country that were struggling with conflict or natural disasters, with the goal to "give children in these areas, who often have little in the way of educational opportunities, a chance to go to school."[13]

Malala's story became important to many people across the world. Supporters cared about the fate of the teen and her fellow Pakistani females. They continued to eagerly follow her progress along with her family, friends, and fellow Pakistanis, who were anxious for her full recovery.

STUDENTS PROTEST COLLEGE RENAMING

Some of the young women at a college in Saidu Sharif renamed for Malala asked the principal to remove the new name plaque from the school. The students were afraid the Taliban would retaliate against the renaming by attacking them or the school. The principal did not oblige. In response, approximately 150 students boycotted classes on December 12. They tore up and stoned pictures of Malala. Student Shaista Ahmed explained her actions:

We feel the college would be the potential target of militants. I joined others who chanted slogans against Malala and pelted stones on her picture because she had left the country to settle abroad. We are poor, we cannot afford it and we will suffer because she has fled to Britain.[14]

The protesters dispersed after local officials promised to pass on the students' demand to higher authorities. Hearing of the protest, Malala called Kamran Rehman Khan, a local government official, and asked that her country not rename the school.

CHAPTER
NINE

UNSTOPPABLE

O n October 9, 2012, a single bullet drastically changed Malala's life. She was critically wounded, which kept her away from school and her family. One week after being shot, Malala found herself in a different country on a different continent.

Malala's care facility, Queen Elizabeth Hospital in Birmingham, used a Web page to keep followers updated on her status. The first entry was made at 9:00 a.m. on Tuesday, October 16. In it, readers learned Malala had arrived at the hospital safely the day before and was in stable condition.

The update for October 17 was encouraging. In addition to noting her condition was still stable, the post said Malala was responding well to treatment.

The longest log was provided on October 19. It listed details of Malala's injury:

- *Malala was shot at point blank range*

Malala, reading in her hospital room during recovery, continues to seek an education undeterred by the Taliban.

83

- *Bullet hit left brow—instead of penetrating skull it travelled underneath the skin, the whole length of side of head and into neck*

- *Shock wave shattered thinnest bone of skull and fragments were driven into the brain*

- *Soft tissues at base of jaw/neck damaged*

- *Bullet carried on through, across top of shoulder and landed above the left shoulder blade*

- *The surgery to remove the bullet was successful and she was moved to the intensive care unit[1]*

The doctors at the hospital had found additional injuries. They discovered the joint of her left jawbone was damaged. Malala also had fractures behind one of her ears and at the base of her skull.

The long entry also said Malala was awake and aware. Other good news was that she had movement in her limbs and had stood with the help of medical staff. But Malala also faced challenges, including being unable to speak because of the tube in her throat. This did not stop her from communicating, however, which she did by writing notes. Malala's brain was still swollen, and she was fighting an infection. She tired easily. Doctors were uncertain how long Malala's full recovery would take, but most estimates were months—or years.

The hospital's Web page included photographs with the updates. The first appeared on October 20, giving the world its first peek at a recovering Malala, who was awake and looking directly at the camera.

Reunited

Malala had not spoken to her family for weeks. She had traveled from Peshawar to Birmingham without them, and she could not speak to them because she had a tube in her neck. Finally, on October 25, her parents and brothers arrived in England. They rushed to Malala's side immediately.

Malala's father spoke with a Pakistani television network about traveling to the United Kingdom to be with his daughter. While he wanted and

FINAL ENTRY

Queen Elizabeth Hospital made its final post about Malala's health on Friday, November 16, 2012. In addition to stating Malala was in stable condition and comfortable, the entry discussed donations.

The hospital's charity had created a fund for Malala. On the day of the post, the fund had £9,982.13, which was more than US$15,000. The hospital explained how the money would be used: "Once Malala is well enough, the charity will ask her how she would like the money to be spent."[2]

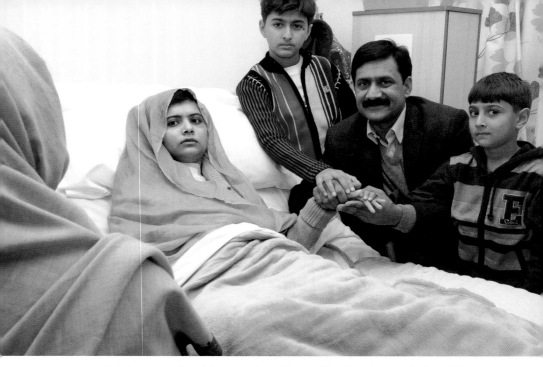

Malala reunited with her family at Queen Elizabeth Hospital: *from left,* brother Khushal, father Ziauddin, brother Atal, and mother, *foreground.*

needed to be with his eldest child, being away from home was not easy. He said,

> I am leaving this country with a heavy heart and in extraordinary circumstances because the whole country knows that it is essential that I be with my daughter during her recovery. With the nation's prayers, she survived the attack and she will surely recover and her health will progress. And, God willing, as soon as she is recovered, I will be back in Pakistan.[3]

Pakistan interior minister Rehman Malik met with Malala's family before they left Pakistan for England. Ziauddin spoke to him of Malala's continual thoughts of

New Year, Continued Terrorism

As 2013 unfolded, Malala and her family were granted new opportunities because of their relocation to England. However, fellow Pakistanis at home faced continued challenges from the Taliban. On February 14, politicians sent out a plea for peace talks with the group after several attacks that day brought more bloodshed. Taliban suicide bombers killed a total of 18 people and wounded 33 others in three attacks in the northwestern part of the country.[11]

CONTINUED RECOVERY AND ADVOCACY: SHAZIA AND KAINAT

Shazia and Kainat, Malala's friends, classmates, and fellow victims, stayed in Pakistan for treatment. On November 29, 2012, the two teens returned to school. Their first day back was challenging. The girls had missed six weeks of school and had to catch up. More than that, Shazia and Kainat experienced many emotions that day. There were hugs, tears, and laughter.

The two young women do not take their school's vehicle anymore. Instead, they commute by motorized rickshaws with a police escort. The teens are protected at home by armed guards.

Even with their return to school, Shazia and Kainat are still recovering from the trauma. The teens struggle with memories of the attack and continue to feel afraid. Kainat does not always sleep well. Shazia wants to be strong and brave to inspire others.

The teens could be angry with the gunman. But rather than speak out against him and the Taliban, the teens chose another path. Shazia said, "I don't want to confront anyone, I just want my education." She prays for her attacker. She explained, "I pray for him to understand that what he did was wrong. Islam gives us this right to get an education."[12]

The Pakistani government's call for peace after these attacks came on the heels of a meeting of Pakistan's main political parties, where politicians had gathered to talk about the ongoing issue of violence in their country.

While such talks were critical, the likelihood of their success was questionable. Previous peace agreements had failed. Still, many felt negotiating may be the only option, since past attempts by the Pakistani military had not ended Taliban violence or broken up the group. Peace talks would prove tricky, given the lack of similar goals between the two sides: the Taliban wants Pakistan to end its relationship with the United States and to put the entire country under Islamic law, and Pakistan's political leaders and its military seem unlikely to meet these demands. With such opposing views and desires, peace talks will undoubtedly be complicated, and Pakistan's future is uncertain.

"We will never be subdued by the militants and their acts. Islam gives us the right to education and we will fight for our rights. We will never ever give up our mission. . . . This land needs us and we can only help Pakistan if we can complete our education."[13]
—Malala Yousafzai, Facebook post on February 7, 2013

Back to School

On Tuesday, March, 19, 2013, Malala attended school for the

first time since the attack. For the immediate future, Malala's school would be the Edgbaston High School for Girls, located in Birmingham. Joining the ninth-grade class, Malala spoke about returning to school:

> I am excited that today I have achieved my dream of going back to school. I want all girls in the world to have this basic opportunity. I miss my classmates from Pakistan very much but I am looking forward to meeting my teachers and making new friends here in Birmingham.[14]

March brought more exciting news for Malala. Late that month, she signed a contract to write a book about the shooting and her family. The book title was already decided: *I Am Malala*, which had become a popular supportive statement across the globe after her shooting. Supporters would hold signs with the phrase at rallies and protests. The book was planned for release in the United Kingdom in the fall of 2013 by British publisher Weidenfeld & Nicolson. US publisher Little, Brown would then release it in the United States and other areas of the world. Malala said of the book,

> I want to tell my story, but it will also be the story of 61 million children who can't get education. I want it to be part of the campaign to give every boy and girl the right to go to school.[15]

The Road Ahead

While she cherishes school and has an opportunity to write a book, for now, Malala's next steps are her recovery. Beyond that, the Pakistani teen's path is as uncertain as her homeland's. What appears definite, however, is that her physical challenges have not affected her spirit. The men who sought to kill her on October 9, 2012, failed. Through her words and actions, Malala Yousafzai has encouraged Pakistani girls and women similar to herself to fight for their rights and seek an education. In the process, she has taught the world the importance of finding a cause, standing behind it, and speaking up, regardless of the risk or response. In April, Malala was named as one of the 100 most influential people in the world by *Time* magazine.

Only time will tell what Malala will do with her life. It seems whatever she chooses, she will succeed, bolstered by a loving family, a legion of fans, and a self-assurance and determination not often found in someone so young.

A smiling Malala on her first day back at school,
in Birmingham on March 19, 2013

TIMELINE

1997
Malala Yousafzai is born on July 12.

2008
In July, the Taliban attacks girls' schools.

2008
Malala joins her father at a Taliban protest in Peshawar, Pakistan, and makes her first public appearance on September 1, speaking against the attacks.

2009
Malala blogs anonymously for the BBC at the beginning of the year.

2009
In January, journalist Adam B. Ellick begins filming his documentary about Swat and Malala, *Class Dismissed: The Death of Female Education.*

2009

The Pakistani Taliban announces girls will
not go to school beginning January 15.

2009

Malala's family escapes Mingora in May. She,
her mother, and brothers live with family members
in exile, while her father stays elsewhere.

2011

On October 25, Malala is named one of five
nominees being considered for the International
Children's Peace Prize 2011; she does not win.

2011

Pakistan awards Malala the first National Peace Award
for Youth in December and renames the prize after her.

2012

Malala is shot in the head by members
of the Taliban on October 9.

2012

Malala's school reopens on October 12 and holds an
assembly to pray for Malala and her injured classmates.

TIMELINE

2012
On October 11, Pakistan police arrest suspects in Malala's attack.

2012
Malala is flown to Birmingham, England, on October 15 for medical treatment.

2012
The first photographs showing Malala in the Queen Elizabeth Hospital are taken and released on October 20.

2012
On November 4, Rehana Haleem apologizes to Malala for the actions of her brother, Atta Ullah Khan, the prime suspect in the shooting.

2012
Malala Day is celebrated on November 10.

2013

In early January, the Pakistani government gives Malala's father, Ziauddin Yousafzai, a diplomatic position in the United Kingdom.

2013

Malala is released from the hospital on January 4 to recover with her family.

2013

On February 1, three members of Norwegian parliament nominate Malala for the 2013 Nobel Peace Prize.

2013

Surgeons operate on Malala on February 2, inserting a cranial plate and cochlear implant.

2013

Malala returns to school, at Edgbaston High School for Girls in Birmingham, on March 19.

ESSENTIAL FACTS

Date of Birth
July 12, 1997

Place of Birth
Mingora, Swat district, Pakistan

Parents
Ziauddin and Toorpekai Yousafzai

Education
Khushal Public School
Edgbaston High School for Girls

Marriage
None

Children
None

Career Highlights
Malala has received considerable attention for her activism. She was nominated for the International Children's Peace Prize 2011 and the 2013 Nobel Peace Prize. In 2011, she was awarded a national peace prize by Pakistan that was renamed in her honor.

Societal Contribution

Malala is an advocate for education in Pakistan, especially for girls. She believes all Pakistani girls have a right to attend school. She has spoken out in support of education for girls on television, in newspapers, and online.

Conflicts

Malala's pursuit of an education and support of education for all people, especially girls and women, has gone against edicts by the Pakistani Taliban. The group considers Malala an adversary because members feel she is promoting Western ways and behaving in an anti-Islamic way. In an effort to silence the young woman, a Taliban gunman shot and critically wounded Malala. After multiple surgeries and weeks of medical care, she is well on her way to recovery, and her message has been spread wider and garnered considerable support from people worldwide.

Quote

"I have the right to play. I have the right to sing. I have the right to talk. I have the right to go to market. I have the right to speak up."—*Malala Yousafzai*

GLOSSARY

activist
Someone who protests or speaks out against a social, political, economic, or moral wrong.

almsgiving
The giving of help to the poor.

assassination
The murder of a well-known person.

burka
A long, loose-fitting outfit certain Muslim women wear to cover themselves, including their faces.

communist
A person who believes in communism, an economic system based on the elimination of private ownership of factories, land, and other means of economic production.

coup
A sudden overturning of power, usually by force.

discrimination
Treating a person differently because of the group to which he or she belongs.

drone
An unmanned aircraft operated by remote control.

exile
To banish a person from his or her homeland.

hepatitis
A serious liver disease that causes fever and makes the eyes and skin turn yellow.

malaria
A serious disease that is passed by mosquito bites and causes fever and chills.

militant
Vigorously active in support of a cause.

patriarchal
A society in which men hold the power.

penal
Having to do with penalties or punishment.

sustainability
The ability of something to continue.

titanium
A type of strong, lightweight metal.

ADDITIONAL RESOURCES

Selected Bibliography

Kneezle, Sarah. "The Malala Yousafzai Saga: Like Father, Like Daughter." *Time: World*. Time, 16 Oct. 2012. Web. 5 May 2013.

Walsh, Declan. "Taliban Gun Down Girl Who Spoke Up for Rights." *New York Times: Asia Pacific*. New York Times, 9 Oct. 2012. Web. 5 May 2013.

Further Readings

Heiden, Pete. *Pakistan*. Minneapolis, MN: Abdo, 2012. Print.

Kovarik, Chiara Angela. *Interviews with Muslim Women of Pakistan*. Minneapolis, MN: Syren, 2004. Print.

Stone, Caroline. *Islam*. New York: DK, 2005. Print.

Web Sites

To learn more about Malala Yousafzai, visit ABDO Publishing Company online at **www.abdopublishing.com**. Web sites about Malala Yousafzai are featured on our Book Links page. These links are routinely monitored and updated to provide the most current information available.

Places to Visit

America's Islamic Heritage Museum and Cultural Center

2315 Martin Luther King Jr. Avenue SE
Washington, DC 20020
202-610-0586
http://www.muslimsinamerica.org
Explore the history of Islam in America, dating back to the 1500s, before the United States was established as a nation.

Islamic Cultural Center of New York

1711 Third Avenue
New York, NY 10029
212-722-5234
http://www.islamicculturalcenter-ny.org
Established in the 1960s, one of the goals of this organization is educating the public about Islam.

Noor Islamic Cultural Center

5001 Wilcox Road
Dublin, OH 43016
614-527-7777
http://www.noorohio.org
Visit the center Saturdays at 11:00 a.m. to learn about Islamic faith and culture.

SOURCE NOTES

Chapter 1. Assassination Attempt

1. "Malala Yousafzai: Schoolgirl Friend Recalls Terror of Shooting." *BBC News Asia*. BBC, 9 Nov. 2012. Web. 5 May 2013.

2. Ibid.

3. Ibid.

4. Ibid.

5. Faiza Mirza. "Voices from the Debris." *Dawn.com*. Dawn.com, 13 Feb. 2012. Web. 5 May 2013.

6. Associated Press. "Girl Shot by Taliban Discharged from UK Hospital." *Yahoo!News*. Associated Press/Yahoo!, 8 Feb. 2013. Web. 5 May 2013.

7. Declan Walsh. "Taliban Gun Down Girl Who Spoke Up for Rights." *New York Times: Asia Pacific*. New York Times, 9 Oct. 2012. Web. 5 May 2013.

Chapter 2. Pakistan

1. "Pakistan." *Encyclopædia Britannica*. Encyclopædia Britannica, 2013. Web. 5 May 2013.

2. "Pakistan Floods of 2010." *Encyclopædia Britannica*. Encyclopædia Britannica, 2013. Web. 5 May 2013.

3. Ibid.

4. Ibid.

5. Ibid.

6. "The World Factbook: Pakistan." *Central Intelligence Agency*. Central Intelligence Agency, 29 Apr. 2013. Web. 5 May 2013.

7. Ibid.

8. Ibid.

9. Ibid.

10. M. Ilyas Khan. "Mingora: Tragic Pakistan Beauty Spot." *BBC News: South Asia*. BBC, 18 Aug. 2010. Web. 5 May 2013.

11. "The World Factbook: Pakistan." *Central Intelligence Agency*. Central Intelligence Agency, 29 Apr. 2013. Web. 5 May 2013.

12. "Rural Poverty in Pakistan." *Rural Poverty Portal*. IFAD, n.d. Web. 5 May 2013.

13. "The World Factbook: Pakistan." *Central Intelligence Agency*. Central Intelligence Agency, 29 Apr. 2013. Web. 5 May 2013.

14. Ibid.

15. Ibid.

Chapter 3. Islam

1. "Muhammad." *WGCU: Islam; Empire of Faith*. WGCU/PBS, n.d. Web. 5 May 2013.

2. Ibid.

3. "Mecca." *Encyclopædia Britannica*. Encyclopædia Britannica, 2013. Web. 5 May 2013.

4. "Great Mosque of Mecca." *Encyclopædia Britannica*. Encyclopædia Britannica, 2013. Web. 5 May 2013.

5. "Q&A on Islam and Arab-Americans." *USA Today: World*. USA Today/Gannett, 30 Sept. 2001. Web. 5 May 2013.

6. "Islam." *Encyclopædia Britannica.* Encyclopædia Britannica, 2013. Web. 5 May 2013.

7. "Islam Today." *WGCU: Islam; Empire of Faith.* WGCU/PBS, n.d. Web. 5 May 2013.

8. "Five Pillars." *WGCU: Islam; Empire of Faith.* WGCU/PBS, n.d. Web. 5 May 2013.

9. "The World Factbook: Pakistan." *Central Intelligence Agency.* Central Intelligence Agency, 29 Apr. 2013. Web. 5 May 2013.

Chapter 4. The Taliban

1. "Taliban." *Encyclopædia Britannica.* Encyclopædia Britannica, 2013. Web. 5 May 2013.

2. Daud Khattak. "New Slaying Highlights Perils Of Journalism In Pakistan's Tribal Areas." *Radio Free Europe/Radio Liberty.* RFE/RL, 3 Feb. 2013. Web. 5 May 2013.

3. Ibid.

4. "Mukarram Khan Aatif." *CPJ: Committee to Protect Journalists.* CPJ, n.d. Web. 5 May 2013.

5. Laura Roberts. "Pakistan: Timeline of Suicide Bomb Attacks 2007–2011." *Telegraph.* Telegraph Media, 13 May 2011. Web. 5 May 2013.

Chapter 5. Birth of an Activist

1. Declan Walsh. "Girl Shot by Taliban in Critical Condition After Surgery." *New York Times: Asia Pacific.* New York Times, 10 Oct. 2012. Web. 5 May 2013.

2. Pamela Constable. "Islamic Law Instituted in Pakistan's Swat Valley." *Washington Post: World.* Washington Post, 17 Feb. 2007. Web. 5 May 2013.

3. Sarah Kneezle. "The Malala Yousafzai Saga: Like Father, Like Daughter." *Time: World.* Time, 16 Oct. 2012. Web. 5 May 2013.

4. Ibid.

5. "Taliban Bans Education for Girls in Swat Valley." *Washington Times.* Washington Times, 5 Jan. 2009. Web. 5 May 2013.

6. "Diary of a Pakistani Schoolgirl." *BBC News.* BBC, 19 Jan. 2009. Web. 5 May 2013.

7. Ibid.

8. Sonia van Gilder Cooke. "Pakistani Heroine: How Malala Yousafzai Emerged from Anonymity." *Time: World.* Time, 23 Oct. 2012. Web. 5 May 2013.

9. "Diary of a Pakistani Schoolgirl." *BBC News.* BBC, 19 Jan. 2009. Web. 5 May 2013.

10. Ben Brumfield. "Malala's Journey from Near Death to Recovery." *CNN.* Cable News Network, 30 Jan. 2013. Web. 5 May 2013.

11. Time Staff. "Interactive Timeline: Malala Yousafzai's Extraordinary Journey: February 2009." *Time: Person of the Year.* Time, n.d. Web. 5 May 2013.

12. Lisa A. Doan. "Malala and Kainat: Voices of Courage." *Georgetown Journal of International Affairs.* Georgetown Journal of International Affairs, 2013. Web. 5 May 2013.

Chapter 6. Exile, Advances, and Honors

1. Ismail Khan. "Pakistan Agrees to Enforce Islamic Law in Violent Region." *New York Times: Asia Pacific.* New York Times, 16 Feb. 2009. Web. 5 May 2013.

2. Adam B. Ellick. "Class Dismissed: Malala's Story (video)." *New York Times.* New York Times, 9 Oct. 2012. Web. 5 May 2013.

3. Ibid.

SOURCE NOTES CONTINUED

4. Ibid.

5. Ibid.

6. Ibid.

7. Ibid.

8. Ibid.

9. Catriona Davies. "Gang Rape Victim Fights Back for Girls' Education." *CNN*. Cable News Network, 21 Feb. 2013. Web. 5 May 2013.

10. Kayla Webley. "Top 10 Everything of 2012: 3. Malala and the Fight for Girls' Education Worldwide." *Time: US*. Time, 4 Dec. 2012. Web. 5 May 2013.

11. "Pakistan Launches Girls' Education Initiative." *UNICEF*. UNICEF, 25 May 2012. Web. 5 May 2013.

12. "Desmond Tutu Announces Nominees Children's Peace Prize 2011." *The International Children's Peace Prize*. KidsRights, 25 Oct. 2011. Web. 5 May 2013.

13. Ibid.

14. Ibid.

Chapter 7. The Unthinkable Happens

1. Sarah Kneezle. "The Malala Yousafzai Saga: Like Father, Like Daughter." *Time: World*. Time, 16 Oct. 2012. Web. 5 May 2013.

2. Ibid.

3. "Malala Yousafzai: Reward Offered for Arrest of Attackers." *BBC News: Asia*. BBC, 10 Oct. 2012. Web. 5 May 2013.

4. Sonia van Gilder Cooke. "Pakistani Heroine: How Malala Yousafzai Emerged from Anonymity." *Time: World*. Time, 23 Oct. 2012. Web. 5 May 2013.

5. Ibid.

6. Mushtaq Yusufzai. "Pakistan Police: Three Arrested over Teen Peace Activist Shooting." *World News: NBCNews.com*. NBCNews.com, 12 Oct. 2012. Web. 5 May 2013.

Chapter 8. The World Responds

1. Ben Brumfield. "Malala's Journey from Near Death to Recovery." *CNN*. Cable News Network, 30 Jan. 2013. Web. 5 May 2013.

2. Ibid.

3. "Malala Yousafzai: Reward Offered for Arrest of Attackers." *BBC News: Asia*. BBC, 10 Oct. 2012. Web. 5 May 2013.

4. Rob Crilly. "Friends of Pakistani Girl Shot by Taliban Vow 'Never to be Subdued by Militants.'" *Telegraph*. Telegraph Media, 13 Oct. 2012. Web. 5 May 2013.

5. Saima Mohsin. "In Rebuke to Taliban, Pakistan College Named for Malala." *CNN*. Cable News Network, 26 Oct. 2012. Web. 5 May 2013.

6. Ibid.

7. Ibid.

8. Rob Crilly. "Friends of Pakistani Girl Shot by Taliban Vow 'Never to be Subdued by Militants.'" *Telegraph*. Telegraph Media, 13 Oct. 2012. Web. 5 May 2013.

9. Saima Mohsin. "In Rebuke to Taliban, Pakistan College Named for Malala." *CNN*. Cable News Network, 26 Oct. 2012. Web. 5 May 2013.

10. Shaan Khan. "Pakistani Taliban Target Female Students with Acid Attack." *CNN*. Cable News Network, 3 Nov. 2012. Web. 5 May 2013.

11. Aamir Iqbal. "Suspect's Sister Apologizes for Attack on Malala." *CNN*. Cable News Network, 5 Nov. 2012. Web. 5 May 2013.

12. Shaan Khan. "Pakistan to Honor Girls Injured in Malala Attack." *CNN*. Cable News Network, 3 Nov. 2012. Web. 5 May 2013.

13. AFP. "Pakistan Plans 'Malala Schools' for Poor Children." *Tribune*. Express Tribune News Network, 12 Nov. 2012. Web. 5 May 2013.

14. AFP. "Students Protest Against Naming of Saidu Sharif College After Malala." *Tribune*. Express Tribune News Network, 12 Dec. 2012. Web. 5 May 2013.

Chapter 9. Unstoppable

1. "Malala Yousafzai Status Updates." *University Hospitals Birmingham*. University Hospitals Birmingham NHS Trust Foundation, 14 Dec. 2012. Web. 5 May 2013.

2. Ibid.

3. Laura Smith-Spark. "Malala's Parents Arrive in Britain." *CNN*. Cable News Network, 28 Oct. 2012. Web. 5 May 2013.

4. Sarah Kneezle. "Malala Yousafzai: Pakistan Taliban Victim's Reunited with Family." *Time: Newsfeed*. Time, 26 Oct. 2012. Web. 5 May 2013.

5. Laura Smith-Spark. "Malala's Parents Arrive in Britain." *CNN*. Cable News Network, 28 Oct. 2012. Web. 5 May 2013.

6. Caroline Davies. "Malala Yousafzai to Have Surgery to Repair Skull." *Guardian*. Guardian News and Media, 30 Jan. 2013. Web. 5 May 2013.

7. "Malala: Schoolgirl Shot By Taliban Speaks Out." *Sky News HD*. BSkyB, 5 Feb. 2013. Web. 5 May 2013.

8. Ibid.

9. Kari Huus. "Malala, Teen Champion of Girls' Rights, Nominated for Nobel Peace Prize." *World News: NBCNews.com*. NBCNews.com, 1 Feb. 2013. Web. 5 May 2013.

10. Ibid.

11. Riaz Khan and Hussain Afzal. "Politicians Talk Peace as Pakistan Taliban Kill 18." *Yahoo!News*. Associated Press/Yahoo!, 14 Feb. 2013. Web. 5 May 2013.

12. Aryn Baker. "The Other Girls on the Bus: How Malala's Classmates Are Carrying On." *Time*. Time, 19 Dec. 2012. Web. 5 May 2013.

13. "Malala Yousafzai (official)." *Facebook*. Facebook, 2013. Web. 5 May 2013.

14. Michael Holden and Mark Heinrich, ed. "Pakistani Girl Shot by Taliban Starts at English School." *Reuters*. Thomson Reuters, 19 Mar. 2013. Web. 5 May 2013.

15. "Pakistani Schoolgirl Malala Yousafzai to Publish a Book." *BBC News: Asia*. BBC, 28 Mar. 2013. Web. 5 May 2013.

INDEX

ABOUT THE AUTHOR

Rebecca Rowell has authored several books for young readers. She has written about physics, weather and climate, wildfires, Switzerland, Iraq, and pioneer aviator Charles Lindbergh. One of her favorite parts of writing is doing research and learning about all kinds of subjects. She has a master of arts in publishing and writing from Emerson College and lives in Minneapolis, Minnesota.

ABOUT THE CONSULTANT

Anita Anantharam is an assistant professor and graduate coordinator in the Center for Women's Studies and Gender Research at the University of Florida. She earned her master's degree in the languages and cultures of South Asia, focusing on Hindi and Urdu cultural history, and received her PhD in South and Southeast Asian Studies, with a focus on women and gender, from the University of California, Berkeley. Anantharam's scholarly interests are in the fields of nationalism and feminism and on women's movements in the United States and South Asia.